POETRY OF LIFE

Poetry of Life

From My Heart to Your Heart

Etta E. Alexander

Library of Congress Control Number:		2015918922
ISBN:	Hardcover	978-1-5144-2599-2
	Softcover	978-1-5144-2600-5
	eBook	978-1-5144-2601-2

Print information available on the last page.

Rev. date: 11/17/2015

To order additional copies of this book, contact:
Xlibris
1-888-795-4274
www.Xlibris.com
Orders@Xlibris.com
729524

CONTENTS

Just For Your Pleasure

Acknowledgements

I am so grateful to my God for His divine favor as He gave me the words to pen in each poem. A big "thank you" to my husband, Rev. David W. Alexander who constantly encouraged me for years to bring forth my writings. To my children and grandchildren who stood with him in total support to push me forward...I thank each of you; I appreciate each of you!

This entire collection was written with "Love and Purpose" and is dedicated to:
My husband
My children
My grandchildren
My godchildren
My siblings
My aunts, uncles and cousins
My church family and Christian growth students
My friends
Persons with disabilities who only need a chance
Young people who need hope
Couples who need encouragement
Parents to say a little love goes a long way
And to YOU, each reader who will also find yourself in the following poems and thoughts.

In Humble Submission,
Etta E. Alexander

Written With Love and Purpose

Where ever you find yourself today; you may be sitting, standing, or lying down. You may be on top of the world; you may be feeling that you are at your lowest point or somewhere in the middle. Know that the reason each poem or poetical writing exists is because of someone like you or me.

The simplicity, yet intensity of each selection is to stimulate and provoke thought and to invite you, every reader into the very pages. I was always motivated to write as a young person, jotting down my thoughts and feelings. Poems have been written on scraps of paper, napkins, envelopes or whatever was found to write on.

It is my prayer that you will be inspired and motivated as you read each poem in <u>Poetry of Life: "From My Heart to Your Heart"</u>; as the individual pieces were *written with love and purpose* - to express love and to remind each person that they have purpose in their own lives. It is never too late – find and live your purpose!

In Memory Of

My Parents
My Grandparents
My Uncles, Aunts and Cousins

CHAPTER 1

FAMILY

You
Are
God's
Gift
To
Each Other…

Make
Every
Day
Count…

"Our Anniversary"

If I could share my very heart
Don't know where I would start

Yes, my heart I will share
For you are always right there

I Love you more than you'll ever know
I honor you and appreciate you so

Thank you for the love you give
And the Godly strength you live

Thank you for your encouraging words
Even when you think I've not heard

It takes a special bond
To hold out until the race is won

We have had our ups and downs
And we keep on loving through the frowns

Thank you for the happy days
That we together have made

Whether on a date or eating out
Or just sitting around in the house
We could be just quiet as a mouse

And feel the love in the air
Knowing that you are right there

Without a doubt to keep me safe
As we honor God in this place

God has plans for us
And in Him we should keep our trust

I trust that you will always know
That I, your wife, love you so much…
Truly David W. Alexander

Written with Love & Purpose
February 26, 2015

"Daughters"

I am blessed and happy on this Mother's Day because I have amazing
daughters!
God blessed me with you
My gifts from Him were you two

To love and to teach all of my days
For the two of you, I am amazed

For what God has done in your lives
And blessed you with such God-given drives

To represent Him in all that you do
To have now children of your own too

To teach and guide
And in the two of you they take Godly pride

You have taught them about God and how to put Him before their goal
So that their life plans would gloriously unfold

I keep praying and thanking God above
Thanking Him for the two of you and all of your love

As we celebrate Mother's Day this year apart
I know you know you are in my heart

I love you, I love you, I love you more
The two of you I appreciate and adore

Happy Mother's Day
Love, Hugs & Kisses

Written with Love & Purpose
May 10, 2015

"Even the Little Things"

A hand-picked flower
A cup of water
A smile
A little hug, sometimes sweaty
The penny you gave full of joy and glee because it was all that you had and
it made you happy
Drawings and writings that came from your heart
We loved you right from the start
Taught you what was right and enjoyed you too
Shower you with love and appreciation, we do
The dreams that you have, we help make them come true
Because we are blessed and thank God for our grandchildren, all of you
We appreciate the love you bring
Even the little things
That makes our hearts sing
Happy songs and praises to God
For His love, protection and guidance and all in between
We thank Him that you will know Him and on Him you can trust and lean
In even the little things

Written with Love & Purpose
May 1, 2014

"I Know the Plans You Have For Me"

Lord, I know the plans you have for me
When I was young, I could not see

We went to church and learned to pray
Mama said keep on, you'll get it one day

No clue about what that meant
On our knees each night we bent

Praying for our neighbors, friends and foes
Mama said one day Jesus would come and knock on our doors

"How is that," I exclaimed
Just keep praying she said, you'll know, you won't be the same

True to her word and to God be the Glory
The words and the life she lived before us told the story

Of Jesus' love here on earth
Through us, He lives …

Thank you Lord, I know the plans you have for me
So all Glory and honor belongs to you

Written With Love & Purpose
May 21, 2014

"Let Them Know You Care"

Today is the day the Lord has made
He blessed you with loved ones, for His life He gave

To all we should cherish and show His love
Not just the ones from whom we think we can get a lot

This and that and whatever it may be
Because when it's too late, you can shout with a glee

You can cry, roll and hollow
But you, they won't be able to see

So while you have time, only one minute or two
A phone call, a short visit and a smile is all it may take

Just to show your loved ones you care and by your actions their day you will make

Let them know you care
Let them know you care!

Written With Love & Purpose
Sunday, 11-26-13

8

"Me, Myself and I"

You've heard the saying – me, myself and I

Me: God's girl, uniquely made

Myself: that's all I can be

I: loving, caring, humble, creative and so very thankful to my God above who made me to be me…all by myself for His purpose so that I can give HIM praise!

Written With Love & Purpose
October 15, 2015

"Mother"

By birth or by another
There is no one like you mother

A whimper or a cry
Always there to dry our eyes

Alphabets and numbers too
The first teacher we knew was you

Time to eat ... to the table we would race
But you paused and made us say our grace

Bible verses and good night prayers
Mother, you were always right there

A fall or a little boo-boo
Your kiss was medicine from head to toe

Chores we did to prepare us one day
When we would get our own pay

As we matured, you would always say
An encouraging word to make our day

Rod of correction you did not spare
For you knew God had placed us in your care

Life may not have always been fair
But your unconditional love was beyond compare

You kept right on praying us through
My God, My God, there is no one like you

The sacrifices you made for us
On your knees in God you put your trust

At church, at school, at home or play
Mother, you taught us the right way

To not lower the bar, but raise it high
We could be anything if we would only try

God blessed you with wisdom and honor to name a few
Character and integrity too

So Mother, we want to say to you
We love you, we honor you, and we appreciate you too!

Happy Mother's Day!!

Written with Purpose & Love
May 5, 2015

"My Sisters and My Brothers"

We had such wonderful parents
Who were our role models
Like a farmer with a green thumb
Six children were in our bunch
And if that was not enough
Cousins, friends or whoever…
There was always someone at the door

Our home was full of love with lots of laughter in the air
We had so much warmth and the best food too

We were always very special in our parents' eyes
And learned the value of a relationship with God
The value of education and hard work
And encouragement we were never denied

As we entered into our adulthood
We find ourselves in different places
So space can never separate our love
Not even across the sea

We may not see each other as often as we would like
But being there for each other, we don't have to think twice

We have always been there to support each others' dreams
And never, never cease to pray for one another
God knew where we belonged and He gave us to each other
So I thank Him every day for you all, "My Sisters and My Brothers"

Written with Love & Purpose
November 8, 2015

"She Grew In Grace"

A blessed baby girl before she was born

She was different from the start
We knew God had set her apart

As she grew in grace...

At the age of two
A house fire and no one knew
With God as her guide, she would be the one who pulled us through

By her persistence and steady tug to awake mother
Only "to God be the Glory" and none other

When she grew in grace...

In school scholarly was she
And like the crowd, she did not want to be

It was always nothing less than Satan putting her through a test
But God's hands were always there and you know the rest

Still she grew in grace...

It's not about her at all
But before the Master she stands tall

Then to do His will, she answered His call
Sixteen years – it doesn't seem like it at all
But she grew in grace

As unto the Lord is her story
It is God who truly gets the glory

As she continues on this life's journey
To preach, to teach and give Godly-wise advice

We give thanks for this woman of God
Daughter, sister, mother, friend, Pastor
And our Father God we do applaud
For all that He has brought her through
The Place Ministries we salute you too
With God in her life, SHE GREW IN GRACE!

Written with Love & Purpose
November 1, 2015

"Show Me The Way"

It's easy to tell me what to do or say
But I look to you to show me the way

It's not about what you tell me to do
Because I am watching you for sure

It's not what you say; it's what you do
That's what I look for to see the real you

I know words anyone can say
But I look to you to show me the way

It's not what you say
It's what you do

I do know that only what I see
Is recorded in my mind to be

Forever a part of me
A part of my life it be

So be careful all you who are "mothers" and "fathers" too
Because your children are watching you

Your life they mimic
And that's no gimmick

So remember it's not what you say
It's what you do

All eyes are watching you
But especially your children too

Show them love
The kind that God gives from above

It's not in how much you give them that they don't need
But it is the time you spend with them indeed

Show them your character each day
So they can use it at work or at play

When they get older, you will see
Some of you in them

So show them love
Show them your character

It's easy to tell them what to do or say
But they look to you to show them the way

Written with Love & Purpose
January 15, 2015

CHAPTER II

YOUNG PEOPLE

**It's okay
To
Be
Outspoken…**

**Just know when and what to say
And do it in the proper way…
Respect yourself…
Choose your territory…**

You are our future!

"ABIDING"

Where are you abiding
Is it in the secret place?

Or is it out in the open for the world to see
Where it is not about God, but "all about me"

When in the shadow of the Almighty is a safe place to be
Oh yes, obstacles may come and you will see
That when you are abiding under His shadow there is protection
That's the key!

So know that there is safety and protection too
He is your refuge; He will take care of you

Where are you abiding
Is it in the secret place?
Under the shadow of the Almighty
The sweet dwelling place

Where He will send even His angels to take charge over you
and others like you
Abiding, abiding, yes indeed, under His shadow
In His safety IS THE PLACE TO BE!!

Written with Love & Purpose
November 8, 2013

"Arise"

Arise to the greatness you can't see
But you know only God created you to be

Arise to behold a brand new day
To face each challenge come what may

Arise to encourage just one more child
Hold your head up and smile

Arise, arise, arise

Whether there are mistakes from your past
Trust in God, and repent
He already forgave you, now relax at last

Arise to praise Him, to adore Him too
Worship Him; serve Him if it's only you

Arise only one day at a time He promises
To do His will so they won't go amiss

Arise to tell His true story, about His love, mercy and grace
So be His voice and hands; use what He gave you and see the love on everyone's face

Arise to know it's not about you
It is only God to whom Glory is due

Arise, arise, arise!

Written With Love & Purpose
November 24, 2013

"A Day in Court"

Life in jail they tell me is hell
But what do you expect
When the truth you must tell

Thoughts in your mind about what to say
For surely in court you will have your day

What do you say, what do you do?
Do the right things

You can sneak and hide
Satan has trapped, fooled you, and laughing at you

Surely one day you will be exposed
Tears and snot will be running from your nose

Only God knows what is true
Oh my God, repentance is needed
If you are sincere and you know before Him one day you'll be seated

To tell the truth you must
Change of heart, change of mind and old acquaintances without a fuss

Because free-will you have been given
So the choices you make, oh well they are your decisions

Right or wrong
Good or bad

You pay the price
And sometimes you pay it twice

You think your day in court is here,
But there is a Judge that is always near

He sits high and looks low
He is everywhere, don't you know

For everything you did or said
Each day in life you make your bed

Life is so short and you can live it well
Just don't listen to Satan and spend your life in hell

Just a sampling of hell on earth
If you let the devil reign in your life

Who is the fool?
When you let him use you, that's not cool

So much better is the plan He has for you
Plans of success and a good life too

Believe in yourself, yes you can
We all have faults but it's in our hand

Learn from your past errors; make it your personal task
You can't go around wearing a mask

Face the world... that you must do
With character and integrity too

Use nothing as a crutch
Only in God, put your trust

Appreciate life at its best
Do the right things; it's a part of life's test

Yes your family will love you and supports you
But only what you do for Christ will surely last

Jesus is there waiting on you
Give your life to Him; that's easy to do

Which Judge would you rather . . . during a day in court?
Choose the right one and life couldn't be better

Written With Love & Purpose
February 6, 2014

"Calm Down My Sister, Calm Down My Brother"

Life may have thrown you some blows
So much rage, where did it come from?
Every time you open your mouth
Sounds like you're mad
What's that all about?

Is it something deep down bothering you?
And you feel no one you can talk to

Life is not meant to be spent in a rage
Sounding like a wild animal who lives in a cage

Calm down my sister, calm down my brother
Take a deep breath

Look in the mirror and who might that be?
Is daddy yelling or mama too?

Is it that teacher who said you'd never be anything?
Is it abuse of any kind?
Or just the friends you picked up over time?

Oh yes, you had to make a point
Cursing and yelling to the top of your lungs

Because you feel you will finally be heard...
Calm down my sister, calm down my brother

Do you know there is a better way?
The Lord will forgive you this day

"Forgive me FOR WHAT... I'm only me"
You were made in God's image and meant to live free

Life hasn't always been fair to you
Now listen closely, let me tell you what to do

Ask the Lord to give you some help
He already knows His commands you have not kept
A forgiver, if you ask Him and it is true
He will direct you in the things to do

Calm down my sister, calm down my brother
It's about you... Now transform that rage and what do you see...

Thank God for that barber, baker, candle maker, designer, architect,
engineer, lawn care business operator, doctor, lawyer, nurse, caregiver,
preacher, plant worker in any capacity.....

You can do it with the right training
YES you and you and you...

When you find yourself loud and in a rage
Calm down my sister, calm down my brother...

You can, you will achieve...
Now just calm yourself down!

Written With Love & Purpose
August, 2014

"Fair"

A favorite saying by most: "That's not fair"...
But Calvary's hill, were you there?

Talk about fair, what did Jesus do?
While on this earth, He ministered to the rich and the poor too

Fair would you call it, as they plotted against Him?
Was it fair when His own disciple forsook Him?

Fair was the silver they gave Judas to betray Him?
Was it fair that with a kiss the Council arrested Him?

Fair was the power He had when even Peter denied Him?
Was it fair that they choose to free a criminal named Barabbas?

Was it fair the stripes He bore on the way to the cross...?
And was it fair Jesus died so you and I wouldn't be lost?

Life is not always fair – but thank God He helped us
By bearing our burden on the cross
So now we can play our part
To see that "the game of life is fair"

Written With Love & Purpose
January 15, 2014

"He Will Change 'Dis' to 'Re'"

He will change…

+ Discouraged
+ Disappointed
+ Dismissed
+ Disdained
+ Disliked
+ Disapproved

As you repent to…

+ Reaffirmed
+ Reconciled
+ Reconnected
+ Renewed
+ Reformed
+ Rejoicing

And your sins will be REMEMBERED by God NO MORE
Don't look back, move forward!

Written With Love & Purpose
October 15, 2015

"Open Your Eyes"

Open your eyes and see the beauty God gave to you

Open your eyes
It's not hard, just try
Possibilities are all around
Don't stay stuck on familiar ground

Open your eyes
Open your eyes and see
All the treasures, all the possibilities
That are there to set you free

If you would only open your heart
Open your mind
And open your eyes
Then all you have to do is try

Open your eyes
To all the splendor
That is outside your four walls
Waiting on you …new adventures, creativity and all

Open your eyes!

Written With Love & Purpose
August, 2014

"Something's a Tugging At My Heart"

Something's a tugging at my heart
Don't know what it is

All I know is that – places I used to go
Don't want to go no more

Things I knew were wrong
Don't want to do no more

Places I used to go
No interest at all

Man, I look at my so called friends
And wonder who will take the fall

But there is something a tugging at my heart
Grew up knowing from the start

That Jesus died for you and me
Mama and Daddy taught me you see

Go back in my mind and wonder
Where did I get off track and felt like I was going under

Thank God for the lessons learned
For salvation cannot be earned

I confessed with my mouth that The Lord
Jesus Christ made the ultimate sacrifice

I believe in my heart
Oh the tugging starts

Something is a tugging at my heart.......

There is one thing that is true
Christ is the answer for you and me

Written With Love & Purpose
February 8, 2014

"Time Out"

Time out for wasting time
Thinking you can hurry and do "it" on a dime

Time out for lying and deceiving yourself
For the Savior you hope to meet

Time out for lack
When you learn that He has everything you need

The Lord is coming soon
So repent and come a running
Back to the only one who can save you man or woman

Time out from all that stuff
Tell the devil, you've had enough

Time out surely it will be
When one day this life you will no longer see

Time in – right now to make a change
God forgives you when you repent and turn from shame
Boldly give Him your heart
Today, you can make a fresh start

You are a part of His creation.
Time out from the old …
With open arms, come on in…
Embrace something new
For you now will begin to win!

Written with Love & Purpose
May 28, 2014

"What Is Love"

When he tells you, "I love you"

Is it because he's got the money
And from you he wants some honey?

Can you trust him
And on him can you depend

Has he given his life to The Lord?
If not, you'd better think twice

When he says, I will change one day
That is quite easy to say

One day is a long time
When just another excuse he makes

Drop you at the ring of the phone
Wait that's my boy and he is gone

Hold up one minute, where are you going?

Got to do something with my boys
Treat you like some little toys

Respect you he does not
Curse like a sailor drunk on a cot

Says you are too timid and wear your feelings on your shoulder
No way!!! And say it boldly

If no respect you get now
No respect you'll allow

Pack your pride and thank God today
That He gave you courage and showed you the way

Out of a relationship that was not cool
You are a beautiful young lady and nobody's fool

You are a jewel and deserve the best
Wait on The Lord, have faith and He will do the rest

You see He is your friend
And on Him you can depend

To love you and forgive you too
Yes He will do that for you

All it takes is to give Him your heart
And you'll feel a little better from the start

No regrets
No looking back

Because true love is what He gives
Started with His son who went to Calvary's Hill

To pay a debt that He did not owe
But "oh thank God", He loved us so

No condemnation you will find in Him
For those who are in Christ Jesus and walk not after the flesh but after the Spirit

Because He is that loving and He is that kind
I pray that you will hear it
And do it too with that in mind

Remember you are blessed
With Jesus on your side you've passed the test

That's LOVE!

Written with Love & Purpose
February 10, 2014

CHAPTER III

WE ARE ALL GOD'S CHILDREN

**Persons
With
Disabilities
Only Need A Chance to show you
their love and uniqueness…**

"YES THEY CAN"

"Thank God For Helping Hands"

Lord I am your child
I know it, even when it's difficult to smile

Mama and Daddy are amazed to see
A little baby, yes, me

Out of rhythm or out of rhyme
I still don't understand it at this time

I understand all I can
Thank God for helping hands

Books I studied and I didn't know
That I had to be taken a little slow

Patience, love and a smile
Would comfort me for a while

Thank God for helping hands

My parents did all they could
All they thought they could do for me they would

They taught me the basic things to do
They even tried to teach me to tie my shoe

Some things I grasped and some I did not
Some I just simply forgot

Thank you God for helping hands
Thank you God they are my fans

As I grew older you see
New caregivers came to me

To help me with everyday living
And like mama and daddy they keep on giving

Some with love, kindness and patience too
Some I had to tell them I am human just like you

They know I understand
And I thank God for helping hands

As simple as it may seem
I say what I mean

Thank you God for helping hands!

Written with Purpose & Love
May 20, 2015

"Give Me A Chance"

I am unique or different you may say
The same things you require, so do I today

Breakfast for you may be full and come with fan-fare
Breakfast for me may be small, but prepared with hands that care

Give me a chance - things are a little different you see

Decisions you make may come easy
Decisions I make sometimes make me feel a little queasy

Give me a chance and you will see
I deserve the best and just want to be

A part of life and live in this society
To live life with no hostility

Give me a chance

Sometimes I may not understand even a tiny little thing
But I do know and understand when your heart you bring

To help me along life's way
For all you do, I know one day
It may not be from me at all
But surely you can stand tall

I know sometimes you don't want to be there
Sometimes I make you want to pull out your hair

God made me the way that I am
Most times I am as happy as a lamb

Give me a chance
I may even learn to dance

For the things you do
The extra miles you go too

Just to make sure my days are normal as can be
Some days I may not know my head from my knee

Days it may be difficult to do this or that
Or even try to put on a hat

But just give me a chance

Remember just a little bit more time with me
Let me be and you will see

I am a special gift from God above
Yes, He showered me with His love

I am a part of this community, as different as I may be
I am a part of this society

Today I want to shout, praise and dance
And just say "thank you" in advance

I may have some insufficiencies
But let's learn to respect and appreciate each other's differences

Just... **Give Me a Chance!**

Written with Purpose & Love
For Persons with Disabilities
May 20, 2015

A Servant Heart

"Whoever wants to be great must become a servant". Mark 10:43

Today, most of us want to be defined by position, power and prestige…
Living the - it's all about "me" syndrome. Jesus does not measure us by
status, He measures us by service.

Servants need to be Christ-like. Those who serve not based on convenience,
but based on the need of those they NEED to serve.

Servants must be
+ Available
+ Ready to see that there is a need and know what is needed
+ Use what they have – they don't need a lot, use what they have
+ Faithful to the end
+ Remain humble – knowing, it's not about me…… It's about HIM
  and others
As unto you Lord, as unto you….LORD!!!
There are elderly, disabled, homeless and misfortunate persons in need all
around you. Let's look for opportunities to serve and have a servant heart.

Written With Love & Purpose
January 2014

CHAPTER IV

JUST FOR YOUR PLEASURE

To encourage you and give you hope and love

"Faith, Hope & Love"
And the greatest is Love
(1 Corinthians 13:13 NIV)

"Be It a Slave"

A slave to her master is hard to be
When there is not communication you see

Do this, do that
And it is a matter of fact

What the master wants, he gets
Better not voice your opinion, please don't

Shows no concern for you at all
Just try to smile and stand tall

Don't appreciate a thing you do
Looking for another opportunity to be harsh to you

In the same house like strangers you see
Not a word, just leave him be

Words do hurt and the silence too
But know that God is looking at you

How would you feel to have lived so long
And at heaven's gate you hear a song

Who are you, I do not know
You who knew right from wrong

You who did not show love
Think you can live in heaven above

I am love, I gave my son as an example
You chose to hate and misuse ample

Time and time again you had a chance
Just kept on and on while in my word you would glance

How would you feel if the table was turned
What do you think you have earned

Love and forgiveness is what they should do
Should they treat you with kindness too

Or give you the same measure you gave
Be it a slave

Written with Love & Purpose
July 6, 2015

"COURAGEOUS"

The lines are not always drawn straight
But they are drawn and sometimes it's fate

So be strong and courageous

The circle seems to move
Or was it a point you needed to prove

Just be strong and courageous

You may think life isn't fair
Trust only in God He will be there

So when you think you don't see your way
Don't give up do what the word say

BE STRONG AND VERY COURAGEOUS!

Written With Love & Purpose
October 28, 2015

"Faith"

Faith we have heard is not just another word

But an action word that's tried and true
Because obedience is sometimes hard to do

It's not the works we do to earn us faith
It's the faith we have that make us work

First we must believe that He is
And all the universe is His

Created man and woman too
No other God could do it, only you

Faith, Faith in your word
How your story must be heard

Around the world to all your people
Big or small, you made us equal

Take pride in your word, yes we do
Because one day by faith we will see you...

Faith, the substance of things hoped for,
The evidence of things we cannot see

Faith in your word we see
We'll keep pressing on so we can be

Celebrating a new life
Eternally with Jesus Christ

Faith, Faith just a little faith

Faith in your word
Your story must be heard.

Written With Love & Purpose
March 8, 2015

"HOLY SPIRIT REIGN"

As I open my eyes from a good night's sleep
Holy Spirit Reign

First fruit praise from my lips are a must
Reign Holy Spirit

Thanking God for waking me up
It is in Thee, I put my trust
Holy Spirit Reign

Some things get in the way
I continue to press and steadfast pray
Reign Holy Spirit

Give You praise and adoration too
For You are so worthy
Holy Spirit Reign

Even in this Lord, I will not fret
Worry is not for me
Because You have it so I can let it be
Reign Holy Spirit

As I continue on my day never, never cease to say
Thank you Lord for making a way
Holy Spirit Reign

Lord I pray that I will represent You today
That someone who is lost or need a little aid
Will know that for their sins You already paid
Reign Holy Spirit…

Holy Spirit Reign!

Written With Love & Purpose
February 7, 2014

"If I Didn't Love You"

If I didn't love you

I would turn a silent ear
And from you I would not want to hear

The upbringing that we gave was solid and true
When you became grown you said you just wanted to be "you"

In this world so perfectly framed
God even knew what you would be named

Be you, you said – did you not know...
You are unique, God made you so

Satan is still like a roaring lion
Making some feel that they were made of iron

Not true at all, God made you with a loving heart
He knew your gifts right from the start

To your own self first be true
Turn to God, only He can truly help you

If I didn't love you, I would tell you a lie
And watch life just pass you by

Tried everything and what do you see
Same old same old is all it be

Are you tired of the same things
Now try a true relationship with God in faith and see what it bring

I love you and God loves you too
Give your life to God, He will help you get through…

Written with Love & Purpose
August 11, 2015

"JOURNEY TO THE WELL"

We all have moments in our life
When things are not just what we would like

Don't know what it is
One minute things are well
The next minute everything seems to fall

Just look at it as your journey to the well

On your journey to the well
Trust in Jesus to meet you there

Learn to praise God in happy times
Give Him thanks in the difficult times

You need to lean on Him when things are fine
Worship Him in your quiet time

On your journey to the well
Trust in Jesus to meet you there

There is no problem too large or small
He died on the cross to concur them all

On your journey to the well
Live, laugh and love

Live life today
Because life is like a vapor... it will soon pass away

Laugh because it's medicine for the soul
Laugh and be happy as you grow old

Love... this is a commandment God gave
Try it and see, you'll be amazed

On your journey to the well
Remember wisdom, but be sure to get understanding that is swell

On your journey to the well
Trust in Jesus to meet you there...

Written With Love & Purpose
May 25, 2015

"My Sister, My Friend"

It was not by happenstance
Nor was it a game of chance

One day we met
Only by God… did we truly connect

Heart to heart
Right from the start

Through the thick and through the thin
We encourage each other again and again

When we have had to take it slow
A sister's love we would still show

Praying for each other and just being there
For support and to show our love and care

Sometimes serious, sometimes not
Sometimes we talk and laugh a lot

And when silent we must be
We pray for each other some more you see

One thing I know and you do too
Is … I thank God He gave me YOU

Yes… You, Margaret, My Sister, My Friend!

Written with Love & Purpose
October 16, 2015

"Thanksgiving: Even in This Season"

Even in this season of life
In spite of all of the strife

No one knows my story
Or why I still sometimes worry

For my mind, body and soul
Oh my, let the truth be told

Days when I could not tell
If I had died and was in hell

I remember Thanksgiving Day
The only time we would pray

And give thanks for the food
And that too depended on the mood

Bitter days are gone at last
For that was then and is in the past

Thanks I give to God above
For being here is true love

You know a house and yard and all of those things
I know now happiness they didn't bring

You see happiness is not dictated by circumstances or people
Only true happiness comes from above
Even in this season, He shows me His love

For food, for shelter and clothes on my back
Look, I have life and that's a fact

I'm so grateful for health, strength and peace of mind
I'm grateful and I'm doing just fine

I am thankful to see children playing
and new extended family praying

Even in this season, I thank God for every day He blesses me to see
For that... every day is Thanksgiving to me

Written with Love & Purpose
For The Shelter for Women and Children November 23, 2013

"Thanksgiving Day"

Turkey, stuffing, pies and all…
Table set for Thanksgiving Day

Never knew what would follow
How my heart would feel so hollow

But look at me now…

Radiant, smiling, happy and free
For I knew not what was to be

Thanking God for He provided His love
Shelter and provisions from above

Just for me!

Now that's THANKSGIVING!

Written with Love & Purpose
For The Shelter for Women and Children
November 23, 2013

"TIS THE SEASON"

Tis the season to be
Happy

Tis the season to be
Overjoyed

Tis the season of
Expectancy

Tis the season for
Open Doors

Tis the season for
Doors to Close

Tis the season
With a loss

Tis the season
Not so bad

Tis the season for
Acceptance

Whatever the season
Thank God, you are a part of it

AND SEASONS CHANGE!

Written With Love & Purpose
October 13, 2015

"To Win"

What does it mean to win the race
When in the natural you only see

Oh, you did not come out ahead
But when you've given your all
And on the Master you did call
Stayed right there in the race
And ran it with a steady pace

The race you were in may not have been for you
Remember The Master's race and His timing too

Remember Job in the Bible days as he went through it all
On the Lord, he remembered to call

Did you hold out to the end?
Well, you know how and what it means to win…

Written With Love & Purpose
October 18, 2015

"TRUE FRIEND"

We were not created to live alone on this earth
Thank God for giving us friends, true friends, faithful friends

Steadfast, loyal and true
One who knows, just what to say and do
Never rubs you the wrong way and knows just how to treat you

A true friend is a blessing from above
She makes you feel like a hand in a warm glove

Never will she glory in your down fall
But will walk beside you to help you stand tall

Comforting and supportive too
Oh, thank God, for my friend is you

A true friend on whom I can depend at any time
Thank you Lord, she makes you shine

By being Jesus' hands, His arms and feet
Extending love without missing a beat

Thank you Lord for this my true friend
You know I can depend on her

My friend, true friend...
I'm so glad God blessed me with you....

Written With Love & Purpose
February 24, 2015

"Vision"

Look in your heart
Feel it – it's real
Write it down, it comes alive
Learn as much about it, YES
Practice and live it and see it as it grows into REALITY!

Written with Love & Purpose
August, 2014

"What Do You Give"

What do you give from day to day
When you open your eyes, do you begin to pray

What do you give
Lord I thank you for one more day
Thank you Lord is all I want to say
Or nothing you give because you must hurry and be on your way

What do you give
When all is well, do you continue to tell
Of His goodness and His mercy too
Do you tell others that without Him you wouldn't know what to do
Because He really, really loves you

Or only when a situation arises
And to God you must cry
Is that when you call on Him
And quickly make promises

What do you give...
+ Your heart
+ Your time
+ Your praise
+ Your talent
+ And what about your prayers
+ And your listening ear

What do you give?
You decide, for it's up to you

Written with Love & Purpose
August 12, 2012

64

"What Harm Is It"

I smile
You don't

What harm is it?

You bring me along for the ride
But my feelings I must hide

What harm is it?

A person says hello
And you go running out the door

What harm is it?

Is it not true
That the only bible some may see is you

What harm is it?

Can't you see or do you know
Just what the bible says is so

It's not just for the other man
You can believe that if you can

Surely it is for you
Who must honor God too

What harm is it?

Who said you were above the word
That you preached and others heard

God's example you must follow
And not condemn or slander or hollow
Insults that are not so
While you are storming out of the door

What harm is it?

This does not just hurt me
I know you know God can see
What you do is not right
Not even in His sight

I pray that you will one day learn
That for forgiveness would be your concern

And life's not all about you
To God, I pray you will be true

Lots of harm you have done
But one day in this terrible race I will not have to run

Lying and denying your true feelings
Are about you and your dealings

As I sit and write my story
My heart aches and I still give God the glory

What harm is it?

Written with Love & Purpose
May 11, 2015

"A Little Love"

A little love goes a long way
Try showing your love to someone today

Just a smile or a friendly hello
To your neighbor or to someone you don't know

Sure will make the difference you see
Does not cost any money, it's free

Just a smile or a friendly hello
Can make the difference in the day you know

A card or a letter
That may be a little better
Just a way to show that you care
And that there is someone nice out there

Just a little love goes a long way
Try showing someone your love today!

Written with Love & Purpose
May 10, 2014

Printed in the United States
By Bookmasters